THE AUGUSTAN REPRINT SOCIETY

[KANE O'HARA]

MIDAS:

AN

English Burletta

(1766)

Introduction by
P. T. DIRCKS

PUBLICATION NUMBER 167
WILLIAM ANDREWS CLARK MEMORIAL LIBRARY
UNIVERSITY OF CALIFORNIA, LOS ANGELES
1974

INTRODUCTION

Allardyce Nicoll's definition of the burletta as a burlesque comic opera which deals in a ludicrous way with classic legend or history[1] validly describes the English form of the genre, since it focuses on the two factors which most influenced its development: the operatic mode in music and the burlesque tradition in literature. English audiences were introduced to the burletta in its Italian form in November 1748 when Rinaldo de Capua's slight comic opera, *La Comedia in Comedia*, was produced at the Haymarket, "being the first of this Species of Musical Drama ever exhibited in England."[2] The Italian burletta, voguishly continental in its production, was immediately well received and maintained its popularity with audiences who for some time had expected songs and dances to be a part of virtually all productions. Indeed, the Italian burletta successfully competed with other forms of musical drama popular during the period: early English opera, the Italian *opera seria*, English comic opera, and the ballad opera.

Although the Italian burletta borrowed heavily from both its musical predecessors and contemporaries, it was viewed by an enthusiastic public as a fresh new form. Serious English opera, on the London stage since Davenant's *Siege of Rhodes* (1658), though marked by an heroic and often spectacular character, was almost always dramatically insubstantial. With the introduction early in the eighteenth century of the Italian *opera seria*, particularly in the works of Handel, the theatregoing public experienced heroic plays that were strongly dramatic, and soon turned to them in preference to the weaker English vehicles. In form, the Italian differed from the English opera in the use of recitative and aria and in rigid conventions governing the kinds of roles sung and in the distribution of the airs. Italian opera continued for many years as the vogue of the fashionable audience, despite strong criticism from the playwrights, players and commentators.[3]

Lighter English musical drama successfully coexisted with Italian opera on the London stage in the form of ballad operas and, to a lesser extent, comic operas. Ballad opera, a realistic and often satiric form of drama, was composed of prose dialogue interspersed with songs which were usually set to familiar or popular airs. They were performed with few stage and musical effects, but with much spirit in the acting. Gay's *Beggar's Opera* (1728), the first important work of this kind, remained popular throughout the century and was often imitated until about 1750. Comic opera, which was almost prohibitively expensive to produce, appeared less frequently. It required a staff of singers, in addition to the permanent theatre company, since it was built around complicated original music written especially for the production. W. J. Lawrence neatly summarizes the production differences between the two forms: "Ballad opera was designed for the player who could sing, comic opera for the singer who could make some attempt at acting."[4] In addition, comic opera demanded elaborate machinery to accommodate its spectacular stage effects.

The reasons for the immediate popular success of the burletta seem to lie in the simplicity of its plot and lightness of its music. Serious Italian opera, which had virtually driven early English opera from the stage, never attained such popular appeal. Most middle-class English theatregoers found the complicated plot structure of the Italian opera, obfuscated by its being sung in a foreign language, a barrier to enjoyment. English composers and librettists seemed unable to imitate successfully the serious Italian opera, for there was only one that achieved considerable success, and that came late in the century in Dr. Thomas Arne's *Artaxerxes* (1762). In addition, the English sensibility failed to accept the recitative, which characteristically links the arias of serious Italian opera. On the other hand, the burletta appealed to English audiences because it combined the virtues of its predecessors in a much simpler way: (1) it satisfied the same love for sophisticated music as did serious opera; (2) like the ballad opera, it presented low comedy or farce that could be appreciated by even the unsophisticated, despite its being sung in Italian; and (3) it did not use recitative seriously but took advantage of it to achieve comic effect.

From the point of view of production, the burletta was economical to produce since it generally required little stage machinery. It also had the appeal of effective bawdy comedy[5] and was marked by a rapid singing style and a characteristic gusto of performance. Both John Edwin and Anne Catley, who were to attain distinction as burletta singers, were celebrated for the quickness and vivacity of their singing. Speaking of Edwin, Michael Kelly, the Irish singer, remarked: "I knew him well; he was the best English burletta singer I ever heard; he had great rapidity of utterance, and was a competent musician."[6] Miss Catley, whose stage presence so inspired Dublin ladies that they brushed their hair low on their foreheads in imitation of her coiffure and pronounced themselves "Catlified,"[7] was said to be "amazingly successful where the Music is quick and rapid" (*St. James Chronicle*, 13 December 1774). With spirit and style, the Italian burletta held the boards for some fourteen years after its introduction at the Haymarket in 1748, but eventually lost its popularity and was nearing the end of its life on the English stage at the time that Horace Walpole wrote to George Montagu on 26 January 1762, "Our burlettas are gone out of fashion."

Kane O'Hara's *Midas*, appearing shortly thereafter, was the first English play to be subtitled a burletta. Presented on 22 February 1764 at Covent Garden and playing to an audience which applauded it as "a very agreeable entertainment,"[8] it became one of the most popular afterpieces in the English repertory throughout the century. By 1800, it had been performed over 200 times. The 1764 production of *Midas* put new life into the burletta form by creating a distinctly "English" burletta, making use of the English language, English type characters, a host of English and Irish ballads and airs, and a particularly British form of humor. Thus the virtues of both the Italian form and the English manner were combined to establish a popular dramatic genre in the patent theatres.

O'Hara, a gentleman of learning and wit, added yet another distinctive facet to the English burletta: he allowed the French post-Renaissance tradition of burlesque literature to condition the viewpoint and develop the flavor of his play. The age of burlesque literature had been initiated in France with the publication of Paul Scarron's *Le Virgile Travesti* (1648), a lengthy poem which cleverly mocked the gods, goddesses, and heroes of antiquity by reducing them to contemporary types and placing them in questionable and often ludicrous situations. The tradition became more and more deeply established as Ovid, Juvenal, and Homer became the favorite targets of burlesque authors. Theatrically, the tradition was developed by the *Comédie Italienne,* which produced a number of plays in Paris depicting the gods and goddesses in contemporary dress for the purpose of satirizing the manners of contemporary society.[9] The burlesque treatment of gods, goddesses and classical heroes received further impetus and encouragement in the *Théâtres de la Foire* at St. Germain and St. Laurent, where the burlesque tradition became an important part of the developing *comédie en vaudevilles.*

O'Hara saw in French burlesque a likely instrument for attacking the pretensions of society, the pomposities of Italian opera, and the artificial heroics of inflated tragedy. He sensed that the French-born practice of diminishing classical deities would delight English audiences who would be amused by the disparity between the gods' revered places in the mythological literature to which most of them had been exposed while in school and the ludicrous contemporary English situations in which the playwright placed them.[10] In *Midas,* O'Hara burlesqued the classical legend of Apollo's punishment of Midas for his poor musical judgment by reducing the deities to ordinary, sometimes unsavory, contemporary types, and took advantage of the obvious humor arising from the diminution of the characters to create a basis for restrained satire, realizing, as John O'Keeffe was later to point out, that "the burletta style is gunpowder ground to go upon."[11] O'Hara, in *Midas,* thus combined the strength of the French burlesque tradition in literature with the popularity of the operatic mode in music to create a new dramatic form, the English burletta, which became a favorite type of afterpiece for the remainder of the century.

The success of *Midas* was the product of many forces, musical, social, national, and theatrical. *Midas* had originally been written as a slight comic opera intended only for private production for the Dublin aristocracy. As such it had been performed and applauded in April 1760 at the private theatre attached to the residence of the Right Honorable William Brownlow at Lurgan—and was almost forgotten.[12] But the following year, when Irish patriotic pride was threatened, *Midas* was promptly recalled into service. The cause of the crisis was the renowned D'Amici family, a group of seasoned performers who had given burlettas at London's "Marybone" Gardens during the late 1740's and early 1750's. When the D'Amici's successfully brought their production of Scolari's popular Italian burletta, *La Cascina,* to Smock Alley on 19 December 1761, the rivalry between the Smock Alley Theatre and the Viceregent's favorite theatre at Crow Street, which had always been keen, was immeasurably heightened. Lord Mornington, founder and active participant in The Dublin Academy of Music, persuaded his good friend, Kane O'Hara, to adapt *Midas* so as to make it the native Irish response to Italian burlettas.

O'Hara complied by making *Midas* a native Irish burletta: he lengthened his original work to include material specifically critical of the Italian burletta performers and his topical allusions were so abundant that John O'Keeffe later admitted that *Midas* was "made up of Dublin jokes and bye-sayings, but irresistibly humorous."[13] The production of *Midas* as a burletta became a chauvinistic cause for Dubliners and the piece was put into rehearsal with great expectations. It was announced that the music would be conducted by Signior Joseph Vernoni (honest Jo. Vernon), and the actors and actresses similarly had their names Italianized: Pat Mahony became Signior Patrico Mahoni and Elizabeth Glover was announced as Signorina Elizabetta Gloverina. *Midas* was produced at Dublin's Crow Street Theatre on 22 January 1762, with many of the city's favorite singers taking part. It was an overwhelming success.

The process of modification and adaptation continued as O'Hara prepared *Midas* for the London stage. The plot lines remained intact, but many of the Dublin allusions were deleted; words and expressions more significant to the larger English audience were substituted. Some of the humorous passages were subdued; the English audiences accustomed to the refinements of language and tone gradually introduced by Garrick during the previous two decades might not have been responsive to the more robust and earthy aspects of Irish humor. *Midas,* the chauvinistic Irish burletta, had now become *Midas, an English Burletta.*

Midas opened in London on 22 February 1764 with a cast that included Beard as Sileno, Mattocks as Apollo, Shuter as Midas, Dunstall as Pan, Fawcett as Damaetas, Miss Miller as Daphne, Miss Hallam as Nysa, and Miss Poitier as Mysis. The play was well acclaimed, but intelligent play-doctoring was still needed, for *Midas,* as a three-act play, had too little dramatic substance to satisfy an English audience as a mainpiece. When it was brought out again on 5 February 1766 as a two-act afterpiece, it achieved its greatest success. The 1766 edition of Midas, which is the first edition of the two-act play, is reprinted here. It was printed for W. Griffin, W. Nicoll, and T. Lownds. Curiously it is referred to as "The Third Edition" on the title page since two previous editions of *Midas* as a three-act play had appeared in 1764.[14] In its two-act form, it was performed twenty-seven times during the single season 1765-66, once, on 17 February, "by Command of their Majesties."[15] *Midas* was thereafter a byeword to English audiences, with the incomparable Ned Shuter, who was later to achieve renown playing the old men of Goldsmith and Sheridan, especially admired in the title role. In addition to maintaining its position as one of the favorite afterpieces at Covent Garden throughout the century, it was also brought out by Samuel Foote at the Haymarket in 1770 and remained in that theatre's repertory.

Much of the play's success was due to O'Hara's genius for selecting music which would effectively dramatize his literary text. Pol's air, "Lovely nymph asswage my anguish" (I, xiii; see Appendix) sung tenderly to Daphne, is the romantic high point of the play. O'Hara has set the lyric to a popular air, "The Rapture," which was still described, some thirty years later, as one of the "most favourite English songs which have been sett to Music and sung at the Public theatres and Gardens."[16] Marked "affettuoso," it is a graceful melody written with much ornamentation to enhance its romantic quality. By contrast, the air selected to conclude Act I (see Appendix) and to display the spirited argument between the sisters, rivals for the affections of Pol, is a well-known dance tune, "Bobbing Joan," which had been popular for over a hundred years and had received extraordinary exposure by having appeared in five ballad operas: Gay's *Polly* (1729), Fielding's *Author's Farce* (1730), Odingsell's *Bays's Opera* (1730), Worsdale's *A Cure for a Scold* (1735), and Baker's *The Mad House* (1737). One recalls that Fielding's Squire Western had Sophia play this on the harpsichord every afternoon "as soon as he was drunk," although, she, as a young lady of refined taste, preferred the works of Handel.

"Bobbing Joan" lends itself to satirical use and effectively and humorously depicts in music the visual comedy presented on stage as the statuesque sister, Daphne, calls her sister,

"Pigmy Elf," only to hear the petite Nysa retort, "Colossus it self." O'Hara indicates that the air ought to be rendered "allo spiritoso" and sets it in two-part harmony to suggest the dimensions of the argument.

Similarly, the central plot element of the second act, the spoof of Midas' poor musical taste, is conveyed by O'Hara's choice of appropriate music. In the actual contest, Pan sings "A pox of your pother" (II, x; see Appendix), a simple melody of regular structure and little rhythmical or harmonic interest, whereas Pol renders the romantic "Ah happy hours" (II, xi; see Appendix), which is introduced by a pizzicato, ornamented by trills and appoggiaturras, and characterized by varied rhythms. These two melodies, sung in succession, provide the audience with a persuasive and humorous musical illustration of the prejudice of Midas, who proclaims Pan the winner.

Throughout the play, there is a high degree of integration of music into the play so that the music takes on a dramatic function. Thus, in *Midas,* the highest expectations of musical drama are reached in that the music enhances the literary text of the play and conveys its meaning in a way that words alone could not.

As the popularity of *Midas* increased, travelling companies of players began to bring the play to the provinces,[17] as well as to the Irish towns and villages.[18] Even the hardy American theatre responded to this improbable little tale of gods and goddesses. Advertised as "never acted in America," *Midas* was presented at the Southwark Theatre in Philadelphia on 24 November 1769, to an exuberant audience. Three more performances were scheduled during the next three weeks, and, from that time on, the play became an important part of the repertory and was hailed by audiences in that city and in New York, Boston, and Charleston, as well, until the end of the century.[19] Noting the popularity of *Midas,* George O. Seilhamer, the renowned nineteenth-century historian of the American theatre, has pronounced *Midas* "one of the most delightful mythological burlesques ever written."[20] One indication of its great audience appeal is the fact that Mrs. Douglas, the famous actress whom William Dunlap has described as "the favourite of the West Indian and North American colonists from 1752,"[21] chose *Midas* for her benefit performance on 14

June 1773, at the John Street Theatre. Stephen Woolls, the veteran actor with the Old American Company, made the same choice in New York on 2 June 1786. He had long been a favorite in the part of Apollo.[22] The popularity of Midas continued well into the nineteenth century in England,[23] Scotland,[24] and America.[25]

Audiences of many countries thus have responded to the theme, the music, the lyrics, and the humor of *Midas.* Robert Hitchcock, the eighteenth-century theatrical historian, seems to have best expressed the reaction of the eighteenth-century public to the play: "That the Burletta of *Midas,* possesses an extraordinary degree of merit, is universally allowed. It is . . . superior to every one of the numerous productions of that species, which have since followed it . . . . Its success has been remarkable, and it ever will hold a distinguished place amongst the entertainments of the stage."[26]

C. W. Post College
Long Island University

NOTES TO THE INTRODUCTION

1. *A History of English Drama 1660-1900* (Cambridge: University Press, 1952), III, 194.

2. *Daily Advertiser*, 8 November 1748.

3. See John Burgoyne, "Preface" to *The Maid of the Oaks* (London, 1774); Joseph Addison, *Spectator* No. 29; "On Operas and the Force of Music. A Criticism of Addison's 'Rosamond' " (anonymous review), *The British Journal, or the Traveller*, 9 January 1731, reprinted in John Loftis, ed., *Essays on the Theatre from Eighteenth Century Periodicals*, The Augustan Reprint Society Publication Number 85 (Los Angeles, 1960).

4. "Early Irish Ballad Opera and Comic Opera," *The Musical Quarterly*, VIII (July 1922), 399.

5. Paul Hiffernan commented thus on the performance of Signora Nicolina Giordani, who played Spiletta so distinctively in *Gli Amanti Gelosi* that she was thereafter affectionately referred to by that name: "Some over-nice critics, forgetting or not knowing the meaning of the word Burletta, cry that her manner is *outre*. Would she not be faulty were it otherwise?" *The Tuner*, I (London, 1754), 17.

6. *The Reminiscences of Michael Kelly* (London: H. Colburn, 1826), I, 335.

7. The Reverend S. C. Hughes, *The Pre-Victorian Drama in Dublin* (Dublin: Hodges, Figges, and Company, Ltd., 1904), p. 19.

8. *The Critical Review; or, Annals of Literature* (London, 1764), XVII, 312.

9. The plays of the *Comédie Italienne* became available to Englishmen when Jacob Tonson published the famous Gherardi collection, *Le Théâtre italien de Gherardi*, in London in 1714.

10. Even those Englishmen who were not classically educated at the university were apt to be conversant with mythology through the popularity of *The New Pantheon: or Fabulous History of the Heathen Gods, Goddesses, Heroes &c.*, published in 1760. This prose paraphrase of the most celebrated mythological tales went through six editions in twelve years. *The New Pantheon* gave a detailed account of the Midas legend, dealing with Midas' yearning for gold and with his judgment of the musical contest.

11. John O'Keeffe, *Recollections* (London: Henry Colburn, 1826), II, 347.

12. William H. Grattan Flood, *A History of Irish Music* (Dublin: Browne and Nolan Limited, 1906), p. 299.

13. O'Keeffe, I, 52.

14. Four editions subsequent to that of 1766, all by the same printer, evidence few changes, none of them significant. The last edition printed in the century, that of 1787, has little authority since it was printed five years after the author's death and was done by a new printer, G. Lister. The 1787 edition seriously violates the intention of the author in that it does not mention the recitative, nor does it separate airs from the dialogue; it thus misrepresents the play as a light comedy, wholly in dialogue.

15. Performance records are drawn from *The London Stage 1660-1800*. Part 4 (1747-1776), ed. with a critical "Introduction" by George Winchester Stone, Jr. (Carbondale, Illinois: Southern Illinois University Press, 1962).

16. "The Rapture" was printed in *The Bull-finch. Being a Choice Collection of the Newest and Most Favourite English Songs which Have Been Sett to Music and Sung at the Public Theatres and Gardens* (London, ca. 1792).

17. Eric Walter White has commented on the productions of *Midas* that were brought to Bristol during 1768 and 1769 and has written persuasively on the influence that *Midas* had on Thomas Chatterton, who began writing a burletta, *Amphitryon*, on 12 August 1769. Although this work was never completed, material from it was incorporated into Chatterton's burletta, *The Revenge*, which was written the following year. ("Chatterton and the English Burletta," *Review of English Studies*, IX [1958], 43-48). Alfred Loewenberg states that *Midas* was reduced to a one-act interlude and presented as such at Richmond on 8 September 1766, but there is no printed or manuscript documentation to support this claim (*Annals of Opera 1597-1940* [Geneva: Societas Bibliographica, 1955], I, 256).

18. W. S. Clarke lists forty-one performances of *Midas* from 1765 to 1794 in the county towns, including Belfast, Kilkenny, Limerick, Derry, Cork, and Newry, observing that "Kane O'Hara outdid all other composers of the burletta." (William Smith Clark, *The Irish Stage in the County Towns 1720 to 1800* [Oxford: The Clarendon Press, 1965], pp. 325, 327).

19. Loewenberg, I, 256. Additional information on American productions of *Midas* may be obtained from George O. Seilhamer, *History of the American Theatre*. 3 vols. (Philadelphia: Globe Printing House, 1888); Rita Susswein Gottesman, ed. *The Arts and Crafts in New York, I, 1727-1776* (New York: New York Historical Society, 1938, 313-14); Thomas Clark Pollock, *The Philadelphia Theatre in the Eighteenth Century* (Philadelphia: University of Pennsylvania Press, 1933); William Dunlap, *A History of the American Theatre* (New York: J. and J. Harper, 1832); Joseph N. Ireland, *Records of the New York Stage*, 2 vols. (New York: T. H. Morrell, 1866-67); George C. D. Odell, *Annals of the New York Stage*, 16 vols. (New York: Columbia University Press, 1927); and William W. Clapp, Jr., *A Record of the Boston Stage* (New York: J. Munroe and Co., 1853).

20. Seilhamer, I, 270.

21. Dunlap, *History of the American Theatre*, p. 57.

22. Seilhamer, II, 181; I, 313.

23. *Midas* was produced at Drury Lane on 25 October 1802 with Michael Kelly taking the part of Apollo. It was again produced on 17 September 1812 at Covent Garden where Sinclair played Apollo. A later English production was at Brighton on 30 July 1859 (*Grove's Dictionary of Music and Musicians*, 5th edition, ed. Eric Blom, 10 vols. [New York: St. Martin's Press, 1955-61], V, 743-44; Loewenberg, I, 256). Edward T. Byrnes, *The English Burletta 1750-1800* (unpublished dissertation, New York University, 1967), notes that *Midas* was performed 54 times during the 1812-13 season. He also cites 56 playbills held by the New York Public Library of Performing Arts (including 17 from the 1812-1813 season) for performances of *Midas* from 1812 through 1859. He thus records a total of 93 performances of *Midas* from 1812 through 1859 (pp. 175-76).

24. Laurence Irving's biography of his grandfather, Henry Irving, the renowned English actor, tells of his having played Jupiter in a Scottish production of *Midas* sometime between September 1856 and September 1859 (*Henry Irving* [New York: The MacMillan Company, 1952], p. 690).

25. Loewenberg cites a revival of *Midas* in Philadelphia on 1 May 1840 (I, 256).

26. Robert Hitchcock, *An Historical View of the Irish Stage* (Dublin, 1788), II, 93.

BIBLIOGRAPHICAL NOTE

The facsimile of *Midas: an English Burletta* (1766) is reproduced from a copy of the first edition of the two-act version (Shelf Mark: NCO/p.v./157) in the New York Public Library. The facsimiles of the four Airs discussed in the Introduction (I, xiii; I, xv; II, x; and II, xi) are included in an Appendix and are reproduced from a copy of the score entitled *Midas. A comic opera as it is perform'd at the Theatre Royal in Covent-Garden* [ca. 1764] (Shelf Mark: M/1503/M48/Cage) in the Folger Shakespeare Library.

MIDAS:

AN

English Burletta.

In TWO ACTS.

As it is performed, at the

THEATRE-ROYAL

IN

COVENT-GARDEN.

THE THIRD EDITION.

LONDON:

Printed for W. GRIFFIN, in Catharine-Street; W. NICOLL, in St. Paul's Church-Yard; and T. LOWNDS, in Fleet-Street.

MDCCLXVI.

[Price One Shilling.]

Dramatis Personæ.

Jupiter,	Mr. Legg.
Juno,	Mrs. Stevens.
Apollo,	Mr. Mattocks.
Pan,	Mr. Dunſtall.

M O R T A L S.

Midas,	Mr. Shuter.
Damætas,	Mr. Dibdin.
Sileno,	Mr. Beard.
Myſis,	Miſs Poitier.
Daphne,	Mrs. Baker.
Nyſa,	Mrs. Mattocks.

SCENE, *firſt on* Mount Olympus, *afterwards on the paſtures of* Lydia.

MIDAS.

ACT I.

SCENE I.

The curtain rising discovers the Heathen Deities, seated amidst the clouds, in full council: they address *Jupiter* in Chorus, accompanied by all the instruments.

Chorus of all the Gods.

JOVE, in his chair,
Of the sky Lord-May'r,
With his nods
Men and Gods
Keeps in awe,
When he winks
Heaven shrinks,
When he speaks
Hell squeaks,
Earth's globe is but his taw.
Cock of the school
He bears despotic rule,
His word
Tho' absurd
Must be law.

Even

Even fate
Tho' ſo great,
Muſt not prate,
His bald pate
Jove would cuff,
He's ſo bluff,
For a ſtraw.
Cow'd deities
Like mice, in cheeſe
To ſtir muſt ceaſe,
Or gnaw.

Jup. (riſing.) Immortals, you have heard your plaintive ſover'n
And culprit Sol's high crimes. Shall we who govern
Brook ſpies upon us? Shall Apollo trample
On our commands? We'll make him an example.
As for you, Juno, curb your prying temper, or
We'll make you to your coſt, know—we're your emperor.

Juno. I'll take the law. *(to Jup.)* My proctor, with a ſummons
Shall cite you, ſir, t'appear at Doctor's Commons.

Jup. Let him—but firſt I'll chaſe from Heaven yon varlet.

Juno. What, for detecting you and your vile harlot?

AIR II.

Think not lewd Jove
Thus to wrong my chaſte love,
For ſpite of your rakehelly godhead,
By day and by night,
Juno will have her right,
Nor be, of dues nuptial, defrauded.
I'll ferrit the haunts
Of your female gallants,
In vain you in darkneſs encloſe them,
Your favourite jades,
I'll plunge to the ſhades,
Or into cows metamorphoſe them.

Jup.

Jup. Peace termagant, I ſwear by Styx—our thunder
Shall hurl him to the earth, nay never wonder,
I've ſworn it gods.
Apollo. Hold, hold, have patience
Papa—No bowels for your own relations!

AIR III.

Be by your friends adviſed,
Too harſh, too haſty dad!
Maugre your bolts, and wiſe head,
The world will think you mad.

What worſe can Bacchus teach men,
His roaring bucks, when drunk,
Then break the lamps, beat watchmen
And ſtagger to ſome punk.

Jup. You ſaucy ſcoundrel—there ſir—come Diſorder,
Down Phœbus, down to earth, we'll hear no farther.
Roll, thunders, roll; blue lightnings flaſh about him,
The blab ſhall find our ſky can do without him.

Thunder and lightning. Jupiter darts a bolt at him, he falls.—Jupiter re-aſſumes his throne, and the Gods all aſcend together, ſinging the initial chorus.

Jove in his chair, &c.

SCENE

SCENE II.

A champaign country with a distant village; violent storm of thunder and lightning. A shepherd sleeping in the field is roused by it and runs away frighted, leaving his cloak, hat, and guittar, behind him. Apollo (as cast from heaven) falls to the earth, with a rude shock, and lies for a while stunn'd: at length he begins to move, rises, advances, and looking forward speaks. After which, enter to him Sileno.

Apol. Zooks! what a crush! a pretty decent tumble!
Kinp usage, Mr. Jove—sweet sir your humble.
Well, down I am;—no bones broke—tho' sore pepper'd!
Here doom'd to stay.—What can I do?—turn shepherd. [*Puts on the cloak, &c.*
A lucky thought.—In this disguise, Apollo
No more, but *Pol* the swain, some flock I'll follow.
Nor doubt I, with my voice, guittar, and person,
Among the nymphs to kick up some diversion.

Sileno. Whom have we here! a sightly clown!—and sturdy:
Hum—plays, I see, upon the hurdy-gurdy.
Seems out of place—a stranger,—all in tatters,
I'll hire him—he'll divert my wife and daughters.
—Whence, and what art thou boy?

Pol. An orphan lad, sir!
Pol. is my name;—a shepherd once my dad, sir;
I'th' upper parts here—tho' not born to serving,
I'll now take on, for faith I'm almost starving.

Sileno. You've drawn a prize i'th' lottery.—So have I too;
Why,—I'm the master you could best apply to.

AIR

AIR IV.

Since you mean to hire for ſervice,
Come with me, you jolly dog;
You can help to bring home harveſt,
Tend the ſheep, and feed the hog.
Fa la la.

With three crowns, your ſtanding wages,
You ſhall daintily be fed;
Bacon, beans, ſalt beef, cabbages,
Butter-milk, and oaten-bread.
Fa la la.

Come ſtrike hands, you'll live in clover,
When we get you once at home,
And when daily labour's over
We'll all dance to your ſtrum, ſtrum.
Fa la la.

Pol. *I ſtrike hands, I take your offer,*
Farther on I may fare worſe;
Zooks, I can no longer ſuffer
Hungry guts, and empty purſe.
Fa la la.

Sil. *Do, ſtrike hands; 'tis kind I offer;*
Pol. *I ſtrike hands, and take your offer;*
Sil. *Farther ſeeking you'll fare worſe;*
Pol. *Farther on I may fare worſe.*
Sil. *Pity ſuch a lad ſhould ſuffer;*
Pol. *Zooks, I can no longer ſuffer,*
Sil. *Hungry guts, and empty purſe.*
Pol. *Hungry guts, and empty purſe.*
Fa la la.

Exeunt, dancing, and ſinging.

SCENE III.

SILENO'S Farm Houſe.

Enter Daphne *and* Nyſa, Myſis *following behind.*

Daph. But *Nyſa*, how goes on ſquire Midas' courtſhip?

Nyſ. Your ſweet *Damætas*, pimp to his great worſhip,
Brought me from him a purſe; — but the conditions—
—I've cur'd him, I believe of ſuch commiſſions.

Daph. The moon-calf! This muſt blaſt him with my father.

Nyſ. Right. So we're rid of the two frights together.

Both. Ha! ha! ha!—Ha! ha! ha!

Myſ. Hey-day! what mare's neſt's found?—For ever grinning:
Ye rantipoles—it's thus you mind your ſpinning?

AIR V.

Girls are known
To miſchief prone,
If ever they be idle.
Who would rear
Two daughters fair,
Muſt hold a ſteady bridle:
For here they ſkip,
And there they trip,
And this and that way ſidle.
Giddy maids,
Poor ſilly jades,
All after men are gadding;
They flirt pell-mell,
Their train to ſwell,
To coxcomb, coxcomb adding:
To ev'ry fop
They're cock-a-hoop
And ſet their mothers madding.

SCENE

SCENE IV.

Enter Sileno *introducing* Pol.

Sil. Now, dame, and girls, no more let's hear you grumble
At too hard toil:—I chanc'd, just now, to tumble
On this stout drudge,—and hir'd him—fit for labour.
To'm lad—then he can play, and sing, and caper.

Mys. Fine rubbish to bring home, a strolling thrummer!
(*to* Pol) What art thou good for? speak, thou ragged mummer.

Nys. Mother, for shame—

Mys. Peace, saucebox, or I'll maul you.

Pol. Goody, my strength and parts you under value.
For his and your work, I am brisk and handy.

Daph. A sad cheat else—

Mys. What you jack-a-dandy?

AIR VI.

Pray, goody, please to moderate the rancour of your tongue:
Why flash those sparks of fury from your eyes?
Remember when the judgment's weak, the prejudice is strong.
A stranger why will you despise?
Ply me
Try me
Prove, ere you deny me:
If you cast me
Off, you blast me
Never more to rise.

SCENE V.

Enter Mysis, Sileno, Nysa, Daphne.

Mys. Sirrah, this insolence deserves a drubbing.

Nys. With what sweet temper he bears all her snubbing! (*aside*)

Sil. Oons, no more words---go boy and get your dinner.

SCENE VI.

Fye, why ſo croſs grain'd to a young beginner?

Nyſ. So modeſt!

Daph. So genteel!

Sil. (*to Myſ.*) Not pert, nor lumpiſh.

Myſ. Would he were hang'd!

Nyſ. and *Daph.* La! mother why ſo frumpiſh?

AIR VII.

Nyſ. *Mama, how can you be ſo ill-natur'd,*
To the gentle, handſome ſwain?
Daph. *To a lad, ſo limb'd, ſo featur'd,*
Sure 'tis cruel to give pain.
Sure 'tis cruel, &c.
Myſ. *Girls for you my fears perplex me,*
I'm alarm'd on your account:
Syl. *Wiſe, in vain you teize and vex me,*
I will rule depend upon't.
Nyſ. *Ah! ah!*
Daph. *Mama!*
Nyſ. and Daph. } *Mama, how can you be ſo ill-natur'd,*
Ah, ah, to a lad ſo limb'd and featur'd?
Nyſ. and Daph. } *To the gentle, handſome ſwain,*
Sure 'tis cruel to give pain;
Nyſ. and Daph. } *Sure 'tis cruel to give pain,*
To the gentle, handſome ſwain.
Myſ. *Girls, for you my fears perplex me,*
I'm alarm'd on your account.
Sil. *Wiſe, in vain you teize and vex me,*
I will rule depend upon t.
Nyſ. } *Mama*
Myſ. } *Pſha! Pſha!*
Daph. } *Papa*
Sil. } *Ah! ah!*
Daph. } *Mama, how can you be ſo ill-natur'd,*
Sil. } *Pſha, pſha, you muſt not be ſo ill-natur'd;*
Nyſ. } *Ah, ah, to a lad ſo limb'd, ſo featur'd?*

Daph.

Daph. ⎫ *To the gentle handsome swain,*
Sil. ⎪ *He's a gentle handsome swain.*
Nys. ⎬ *Sure 'tis cruel to give pain.*
Mys. ⎭ *'Tis my pleasure to give pain.*
Daph. ⎫ *Sure 'tis cruel to give pain,*
Sil. ⎪ *He's a gentle handsome swain.*
Nys. ⎬ *To the gentle handsome swain.*
Mys. ⎭ *To your odious fav'rite swain.*

SCENE VII.

Enter Midas *and* Damætas.

Mid. Nysa, you say, refus'd the guineas British.

Dam. Ah! please your worship—she is wond'rous skittish.

Mid. I'll have her, cost what 'twill. Odsbobs—I'll force her—

Dam. The halter—

Mid. As for madam, I'll divorce her.—
Some favoured lout in cog our bliss opposes.

Dam. Ay, *Pol*, the hind, puts out of joint our noses.

Mid. I've heard of that *Pol's* tricks,—of his sly tampering
To fling poor *Pan*, but I'll soon send him scampering.
'Sblood, I'll commit him—drive him to the gallows!
Where is old *Pan?*

Dam. Tipling, Sir, at th' ale-house.

Mid. Run, fetch him—we shall hit on some expedient—
To rout this *Pol*.

Dam. I fly; *(going returns)* Sir, your obedient.

Exit.

SCENE

SCENE VIII.

Mid. What boots my being Squire,
Justice of Peace, and Quorum;
Church-warden---Knight o'th' shire,
And Custos Rotulorum;
If saucy little *Nysa*'s heart rebellious,
My squireship slights, and hankers after fellows?

AIR VIII.

Shall a paltry clown, not fit to wipe my shoes,
Dare my amours to cross?
Shall a peasant minx, when justice Midas *wooes,*
Her nose up at him toss?
No: I'll kidnap—then possess her.
I'll sell her Pol *a slave, get mundungus in exchange;*
So glut to the height of pleasure
My love and my revenge.
No, I'll kidnap, &c. Exit.

SCENE IX.

Pan is discover'd sitting at a table, with a tankard, pipes, and tobacco before him, his bagpipes lying by him.

AIR IX.

Pan. *Jupiter wenches and drinks,*
He rules the roast in the sky,
Yet he's a fool if he thinks
That he's as happy as I.
Juno rates him
And grates him,
And leads his highness a weary life;
I have my lass,
And my glass,
And strole a batchelor's merry life.

Let him fluster
And bluster,
Yet cringe to his harridan's furbella;
To my fair tulips,
I glew lips,
And clink the cannikin here below.

SCENE X.

DAMETAS, PAN.

Dam. There sits the old soaker——his pate troubling little
How the world wags—so he gets drink and vittle:
Hoa, master Pan—Gad you've trod on a thistle!
You may pack up your all, sir, and go whistle.
The wenches have turn'd tail---to yon buck-ranter,
Tickled by his guittar---they scorn your chanter.

AIR X.

All around the maypole how they trot,
Hot
Pot,
And good ale have got;
Routing,
Shouting,
At you flouting,
Fleering,
Jeering,
And what not.
There is old Sileno *frisks like a mad*
Lad
Glad
To see us sad,
Cap'ring,
Vap'ring,
While Pol, *scraping,*
Coaxes
The lasses
As he did the dad.

SCEN

SCENE XI.

MYSIS, PAN.

Myſ. O Pan! the devil to pay—both my fluts frantic!
Both in their tantrums, for yon cap'ring antic.
But I'll go ſeek 'em all—and if I find 'em,
I'll drive 'em—as if Old Nick were behind 'em.
Going.

Pan. Soa, ſoa—don't flounce;
Avaſt—diſguiſe your fury.
Pol we ſhall trounce.
Midas is judge and jury.

AIR XI.

Myſ. *Sure I ſhall run with vexation diſtracted,*
To ſee my purpoſes thus counteracted!
This way or that way, or which way ſoever,
All things run contrary to my endeavour.
Daughters projecting
Their ruin and ſhame,
Fathers neglecting
The care of their fame;
Nurſing in boſom a treacherous viper;
Here's a fine dance—but 'tis he pays the piper.
[Exeunt.

SCENE XII.

A wood and lawn, near Sileno's *farm, flocks grazing at a diſtance,---a tender ſlow ſymphony.* Daphne *croſſes melancholic and ſilent;* Nyſa *watching her.*
[*Then* Daphne *returns running.*

Nyſa. O ho'! is it ſo—Miſs *Daphne* in the dumps?
Mum—ſnug's the word—I'll lead her ſuch a dance
Shall make her ſtir her ſtumps.
To all her ſecret haunts,
Like her ſhadow, I'll follow and watch her:
And, faith, mama ſhall hear on't if I catch her.
[*retires.*

Daph. La; how my heart goes pit-a-pat! what thumping
E'er ſince my father brought us home this bumpkin.

AIR XII.

He's as tight a lad to ſee to,
As e'er ſtept in leather ſhoe,
And, what's better, he'll love me too,
And to him I'll prove true blue.

Tho' my ſiſter caſts a Hawk's eye
I defy what ſhe can do,
He o'erlook'd the little doxy,
I'm the girl he means to woo.

Hither I ſtole out to meet him,
He'll no doubt, my ſteps purſue,
If the youth prove true, I'll fit him;
If he's falſe,—I'll fit him too.

SCENE XIII.

Daphne, Pol.

Pol. Think o' the Devil—'tis ſaid,
He's at your ſhoulder—
This wench was running in my head,
And pop—behold her.

AIR XIII.

Lovely nymph aſſwage my anguiſh;
At your feet a tender ſwain
Prays you will not let him languiſh,
One kind look would eaſe his pain.
Did you know the lad who courts you
He not long needs ſue in vain;
Prince of ſong, of dance, of ſports---you
Scarce will meet his like again.

 Daph.

Daph. Sir; you're ſuch an oglio,
Of perfection in folio,
No damſel can reſiſt you:
Your face ſo attractive,
Limbs ſo ſupple and active,
That by this light,
At the firſt ſight,
I could have run and kiſs'd you.

AIR XIV.

If you can caper, as well as you modulate,
With the addition of that pretty face,
Pan, who was held by our ſhepherds a God o' late;
Will be kick'd out, and you ſet in his place.

His beard ſo frowſy, his geſtures ſo awkward are,
And his bagpipe has ſo drowſy a drone,
That if they find you, as I did, no backwarder,
You may count on all the girls as your own.

Myſ. (from within) Pol, Pol, make haſte, come hither.
Pol. Death, what a time to call,
Oh! rot your old lungs of leather.
B'ye *Daph,*
Daph. B'ye *Pol.*

SCENE XIV.

Nyſa, Daphne.

Nyſ. Marry come up, forſooth,
Is't me, you forward vixen,
You chooſe to play your tricks on;
And could your liquoriſh tooth
Find none but my ſweetheart to fix on?
Daph. Marry come up again,
Indeed; my dirty couſin!
Have you a right to every ſwain?
Nyſ. Ay, tho' a dozen.

AIR XV.

Daph. *My minikin miss, do you fancy that* Pol
Can ever be caught by an infant's dol?
Nys. *Can you, miss Maypole, suppose he will fall*
In love with the giantess of Guild-hall?
Daph. *Pigmy elf,*
Nys. *Colossus itself,*
Both. *You will lie till you're mouldy upon the shelf.*

Daph. *You stump o'th' gutter, you hop o'my thumb,*
A husband for you must from Lilliput come.
Nys. *You stalking steeple, you gawky stag,*
Your husband must come from Brogdignag.
Daph. *Sour grapes,*
Nys. *Lead apes,*
Both. *I'll humble your vanity, mistress Trapes.*

Daph. *Miss your assurance*
Nys. *And miss your high airs*
Daph. *Is past all indurance.*
Nys. *Are at their last pray'rs.*
Daph. *No more of those freedoms, miss* Nysa, *I beg.*
Nys. *Miss* Daphne's *conceit must be lower'd a peg.*
Daph. } *Poor spite!*
Nys. } *Pride hurt!*
Daph. } *Liver white!*
Nys. } *Rare sport!*
Daph. } *Do, shew your teeth, spitfire, do, but you can't bite.*
Nys. } *This haughtiness soon will be laid in the dirt.*
Poor spite, &c.
Pride hurt, &c.

END OF THE FIRST ACT.

ACT II. SCENE I.

A Grove.

Enter Nysa *followed by* Midas.

Mid. TURN, tygress, turn; nay fly not—
I have thee at a why not.
How comes it, little Nysy,
That heart to me so icy
Should be to Pol like tinder
Burnt up t'a very cinder?

Nys. Sir, to my virtue ever steady,
Firm as a rock
I scorn your shock;
But why this attack?
A miss can you lack
Who have a wife already?

Mid. Ay there's the curse—but she is old and sickly;
And would my Nysa grant the favour quickly,
Would she yield now—I swear by the lord Harry
The moment madam's coffin'd—Her I'll marry.

AIR I.

O what pleasures will abound
When my wife is laid in ground!
Let earth cover her,
We'll dance over her
When my wife is laid in ground.

Oh how happy should I be,
Would little Nysa *pig with me!*
How I'd mumble her,
Touze and tumble her,
Would little Nysa *pig with me.*

Nys.

Nyſ. Young birds alone are caught with chaff,
At your baſe ſcheme I laugh.
Mid. Yet take my vows.—
Nyſ. I would not take your bond, ſir,———
Mid. Half my eſtate——
Nyſ. No, nor the whole——my fond ſir.

AIR II.

Ne'er will I be left i' the lurch;
Ceaſe your bribes and wheedling:
'Till I'm made a bride i' the church
I'll keep man from meddling.
What are riches
And ſoft ſpeeches?
Baits and fetches
To bewitch us;
When you've won us
And undone us,
Cloy'd you ſhun us,
Frowning on us,
For our heedleſs piddling. [Exit.

SCENE II.

Midas, *then* Pan *and* Pol, *liſtening.*

Mid. Well, maſter Pol I'll tickle,
For him, at leaſt, I have a rod in pickle:
When he's in limbo
Not thus our hoity toity miſs
Will ſtick her arms a-kimbo.
Pan. So ſquire, well met——I flew to know your buſineſs.
Mid. Why, Pan, this Pol we muſt bring down on his knees.
Pan. That were a feat indeed;—a feat to brag on.
Mid. Let's home——we'll there concert it o'er a flagon.
I'll make him ſkip———
Pan. As St. George did the dragon.

AIR III.

If into your hen yard
The treacherous reynard
Steals slily, your poultry to ravage,
With gun you attack him,
With beagles you track him,
All's fair to destroy the fell savage.
So Pol, *who comes picking*
Up my tender chicken,
No means do I scruple to banish;
With pow'r I'll o'erbear him,
With fraud I'll ensnare him,
By hook or by crook he shall vanish. [Exeunt.

SCENE III.

A Lawn before MIDAS's House.

Enter Nysa.

Nys. Good lack! what is come o'er me?
Daphne has step'd before me!
Envy and love devour me.
Pol, doats upon her Phiz hard,
'Tis that sticks in my gizzard.
Midas appears now twenty times more hideous
Ah, Nysa, what resource?——a cloyster.
Death alive——yet thither must I run,
And turn nun.
Prodigious!

AIR IV.

In those greasy old tatters
His charms brighter shine;
Then his guittar he clatters
With tinkling divine:
But, my sister,
Ah! he kiss'd her,
And me he pass'd by;
I'm jealous
Of the fellow's
Bad taste and blind eye.

SCENE IV.

MIDAS's Parlour.

Midas, Myſis, *and* Pan, *in conſultation over a large bowl of punch, pipes and tobacco.*

Mid. Come, *Pan*, your toaſt——
Pan. Here goes, our noble Umpire,
Myſ. And *Pol*'s defeat,——I'll pledge it in a bumper.
Mid. Hang him, in every ſcheme that whelp has croſs'd us.
Myſ. Sure he's the Devil himſelf,
Pan. Or doctor Fauſtus.
Myſ. Ah! Squire——for *Pan* would you but ſtoutly ſtickle,
This *Pol* would ſoon be in a wretched pickle.
Pan. You reaſon right——
Mid. His toby I ſhall tickle.
Myſ. Look, ſquire, I've ſold my butter, here it's price is
At your command, do but this jobb for *Myſis*.
Count 'em—Six guineas and an old Jacobus,
Keep *Pan*, and ſhame that ſcape-grace *coram nobis*.
Mid. Goody, as 'tis your requeſt,
I pocket this here ſtuff,
And as for that there peaſant,
Truſt me I'll work his buff.
At the muſical ſtruggle
I'll bully and juggle;
My award's
Your ſure card,
Blood, he ſhall fly his country——that's enough.
Pan. Well ſaid, my lad of wax.
Mid. Let's end th' tankard,
I have no head for buſineſs till I've drank hard.
Pan. Nor have my guts brains in them till they're addle,
When I'm moſt rocky I beſt ſit my ſaddle.

Mid.

Mid. Well, come, let's take one bouze, and roar a catch,
Then part to our affairs.——

Pan. A match.

Myſ. A match.

AIR V.

Mid. *Maſter* Pol
And his toll-de-roll-loll,
I'll buffet away from the plain, ſir.
Pan. *And I'll aſſiſt*
Your worſhip's fiſt
With all my might and main, ſir;
Myſ. *And I'll have a thump,*
Though he is ſo plump,
And makes ſuch a woundy racket.
Mid. *I'll bluff,*
Pan. *I'll rough,*
Myſ. *I'll buff,*
Mid. *I'll cuff,*
Omn. *And I warrant we pepper his jacket.*
Mid. *For all his cheats,*
And wenching feats,
He ſhall rue on his knee' 'em,
O ſkip, by goles,
As high as Paul's,
Like ugly witch on beſom;
Arraign'd he ſhall be,
Of treaſon to me!
Pan. *And I with my davy will back it;*
I'll ſwear,
Mid. *I'll ſnare,*
Myſ. *I'll tear.*
Omn. *O rare!*
And I'll warrant we pepper his jacket.

SCENE V.

Enter Sileno *and* Damætas, *in warm argument.*

Sil. My *Daph* a wife for thee; the ſquire's baſe pandar!
To the plantations ſooner would I ſend her.

Dam. Sir, your good wife approv'd my offers.
Sil. Name her not, Hag of Endor,
What knew ſhe of thee but thy coffers?
Dam. And ſhall this ditch born whelp, this jackanapes,
By dint of congees and of ſcrapes——
Sil. Theſe are thy ſlanders and that canker'd hag's.—
Dam. A thing made up of pilfer'd rags——
Sil. Richer than thou with all thy brags
Of flocks, and herds, and money bags.

AIR VI.

If a rival thy character draw,
In perfection he'll find out a flaw;
With black he will paint
Make a de'il of a ſaint,
And change to an owl a maccaw.
Dam. *Can a father pretend to be wiſe*
Who his friends good advice will deſpiſe!
Who, when danger is nigh,
Throws his ſpectacles by
And blinks thro' a green girl's eyes?
Sil. *You're an impudent pimp and a grub.*
Dam. *You are fool'd by a beggarly ſcrub;*
Your betters you ſnub.
Sil. *Who will lend me a club,*
This inſolent puppy to drub?
Your an impudent pimp and a grub,
Dam. *You're cajol'd by a beggarly ſcrub.*
Sil. *Who will rot in a powdering tub.*
Dam. *Whom the prince of impoſtures I dub;*
Sil. *A guinea for a club,*
Dam. *Your bald pate you'll rub*
Sil. *This muckworm to drub.*
Dam. *When you find that your cub*
Sil. *Rub off, ſirrah, rub, ſirrah, rub.*
Dam. *Is debauch'd by a whip'd ſyllabub.* [Exeunt.

SCENE VI.

Enter Myſis *attended by* Daphne *and* Nyſa.

Myſ. Soh!—you attend the tryal,—we ſhall drive hence
Your vagabond——

Sil. I ſmoke your foul contrivance.

Daph. Ah *Ny*, our fate depends upon this iſſue—

Nyſ. Daph.—for your ſake, my claim I here forego.
And with your *Pol* much joy I wiſh you.

Daph. O, gemini, ſay'ſt thou me ſo?
Dear creature let me kiſs you.

Nyſ. Let's kneel, and beg his ſtay, papa will back us.

Daph. Mama will ſtorm.

Nyſ. What then, ſhe can but whack us.

AIR VII.

Daph. *Mother, ſure you never*
Will endeavour
To diſſever
From my favour
So ſweet a ſwain!
None ſo clever
E'er trod the plain.

Nyſ. *Father, hopes you gave her,*
Don't deceive her;
Can you leave her
Sunk for ever
In pining care?
Haſte and ſave her
From black deſpair.

Daph. *Think of his modeſt grace,*
His voice, ſhape, and face;
Nyſ. *Hearts alarming,*
Daph. *Boſom's warming,*
Nyſ. *Wrath diſarming,*
Daph. *With his ſoft lay:*
Nyſ. *He's ſo charming,*
Ay, let him ſtay,
Both. *He's ſo charming*, &c.

Myſ.

Myſ. *Sluts, are you loſt to ſhame?*
Syl. *Wiſe, wiſe be more tame.*
Myſ. *This is madneſs!*
Sil. *Sober ſadneſs!*
Myſ. *I with gladneſs*
Cou'd ſee him ſwing,
For his badneſs.
Sil. *'Tis no ſuch thing.*
Dam. *Muſt* Pan *reſign, to this fop, his employment?*
Muſt I, to him, yield of Daph. *the enjoyment?*
Myſ. *Ne'er while a tongue I brandiſh,*
Fop outlandiſh,
Daph. *ſhall blandiſh.*
Dam. *Will you reject my income*
Herds and clinkum.
Sil. *Rot and ſink 'em.*
Dam. Midas *muſt judge.*
Myſ. *And* Pol *muſt fly.*
Sil. *Zounds,* Pol *ſhan't budge,*
Myſ. *You lye*
Dam. *You lye,*
Myſ. Dam. Sil. } *You lye, you lye.*
Nyſ. Pan's *drone is fit for wild rocks and bleak mountains*
Daph. Pol's *lyre ſuits beſt our cool grots and clear fountains.*
Nyſ. Pol *is young and merry,*
Daph. *Light and airy*
Sil. *As a fairy.*
Nyſ. Pan *is old and muſty*
Daph. *Stiff and fuſty*
Sil. *Sour and cruſty.*
Daph. *Can you baniſh* Pol?
Nyſ. *No, no, no no.*
Let Pan *fall*
Daph. *Ay, let him go.*
Nyſ. Daph. Sil. } *Ay, let him go.*

SCENE

SCENE VII.

Midas *comes forth enrag'd, attended by a Crowd of Nymphs and Swains.*

Mid Peace ho! is hell broke loose? what means
This jawing?
Under my very nose this clapper clawing!

AIR VIII.

What the devil's here to do
Ye logger-heads, and gypsies?
Sirrah you, and hussey you,
And each of you tipsey is;
But I'll as sure pull down your pride as
A gun, or as I'am justice Midas.

CHORUS.

O tremendous justice Midas,
Who shall oppose wise justice Midas.
[All fall prostate.

AIR IX.

Mid. *I'm given to understand that you're all in a pother here*
Disputing whether Pan *or* Pol *shall play to you another year.*
Dare you think your clumsy lugs so proper to decide as
The delicate ears of justice Midas?

Cho. *O tremendous, &c.*

Mid. Soh you allow it then—Ye mobish rabble?

SCENE VIII.

Enter Pol *and* Pan *severally.*

Oh, here comes *Pol*, and *Pan*—now stint your gabble.
Fetch my great chair—I'll quickly end this squabble.

AIR

AIR X.

Now I'm seated
I'll be treated,
Like the sophi on his throne,
In my presence
Scoundrel peasants,
Shall not call their souls their own.
My behest is,
He who best is,
Shall be fix'd musician chief:
Ne'er the loser,
Shall shew nose here
But be transported like a thief.
Cho. *O tremendous,* &c.

Dam. Masters, will you abide by this condition?
Pan. I ask no better.
Pol. ———I am all submission.
Pan Strike up, sweet Sir.
Pol. ———Sir, I attend your leisure.
Mid. Pan. take the lead.
Pan.———Since 'tis your worship's pleasure.

AIR XI.

A pox of your pother about this or that,
Your shrieking or squeaking, a sharp or a flat;
I'm sharp by my bumpers, you're flat, master Pol;
So here goes a set-to at toll-de-roll-loll.

When Beauty her pack of poor lovers would hamper,
And after miss Will o' the Whisp the fools scamper,
Ding dong, in sing song, they the lady extol;
Pray what's all this fuss for, but---doll-de-roll-loll.

Mankind are a medley——a chance medley race;
All start in full cry to give dame Fortune chace;
There's catch as catch can, hit or miss luck is all,
And luck's the best tune of life's toll-de-roll-loll.

I've done, please your worship, 'tis rather too long,
I only meant life is but an old song;
The world's but a tragedy, comedy, droll,
Where all act the scene of toll-loll-de-roll.

Mid. By jingo, well perform'd for one of his age;
How, hang dog, d n't you blush to shew your visage?
Pol. Why, master Midas, for that matter,
'Tis enough to dash one,
To hear the arbitrator,
In such unseemly fashion
One of the candidates bespatter,
With so much partial passion.
[*Midas falls asleep.*

AIR XII.

Ah, happy hours, how fleeting
Ye danc'd on down away;
When my soft vows repeating
At Daphne's feet I lay!

But from her charms when sunder'd
As Midas frowns presage,
Each hour will seem an hundred,
Each day appear an age.

Mid. Silence——this just decree all, at your peril,
Obedient hear,——else I shall use you very ill.

THE DECREE.

Pan shall remain.
Pol quit the plain.
Chorus, *Oh tremendous, &c.*

Mid. All bow with me to mighty Pan—enthrone him.——
No pouting——and with festal chorus crown him!—
[*The crowd form two ranks beside the chair and join in the chorus, whilst Midas crowns him with bays.*]

CHORUS.

See triumphant sits the bard
Crown'd with bays, his due reward.
Exil'd Pol shall wander far,
Exil'd twang his faint guittar,
While, with ecchoing shouts of praise
We the bagpipe's glory raise.

Mid. 'Tis well !—what keeps you here—you ragamuffin ?
Go trudge——or do you wait for a good cuffing ?

Pol. Now, all attend—[*throws off his disguise and appears as* Apollo.] The wrath of Jove, for rapine,
Corruption, lust, pride, fraud, there's no escaping.
Tremble, thou wretch — Thou'st stretch'd thy utmost tether;
Thou, and thy tools shall go to pot together.

AIR XIII.

Dunce, I did but sham,
For Apollo I am,
God of music and king of Parnass :
Thy scurvy decree
For Pan against me,
I reward with the ears of an ass.

Mid. Detected, baulk'd, and small,
On our marrow bones we fall.
Mys. Be merciful.
Dam. Be pitiful.
Mid. Forgive us, mighty Sol———Alas, alas !

Pol. *Thou a Billinsgate quean,* [*to* Mys.
Thou a pander obscene [*to* Dam.
With strumpet, and bailiffs shall class ;
Thou, driven from man [*to* Mid.
Shalt wander with Pan,
He a stinking old goat, thou an ass, an ass, &c.

Apol. Be thou squire——his estate [*to Sil.*
To thee I translate.
To you his strong chests, wicked mass, { *to Daph.* and *Nysa.*
Live happy, while I
Recall'd to the sky,
Make all the Gods laugh at Midas.

Daph.

Daph.
Sil.
Nys. } *Together with the other nymphs and swains.* {
To the bright God of day
Let us dance, sing and play,
Clap hands every lad with his lass.

Daph. Now criticks lye snug,
Not a hiss, groan, or shrug,
Remember the fate of Midas
Midas,
Remember the fate of Midas.

CHORUS.

Now criticks lye snug, &c.

FINIS.

APPENDIX

Sung by Mr Mattocks

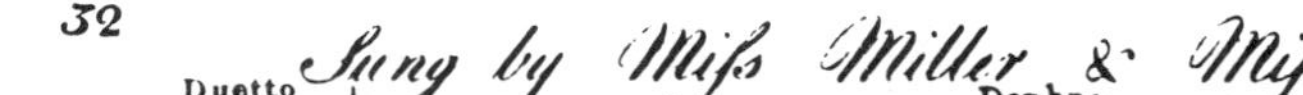

Sung by Miss Miller & Miss Hallam

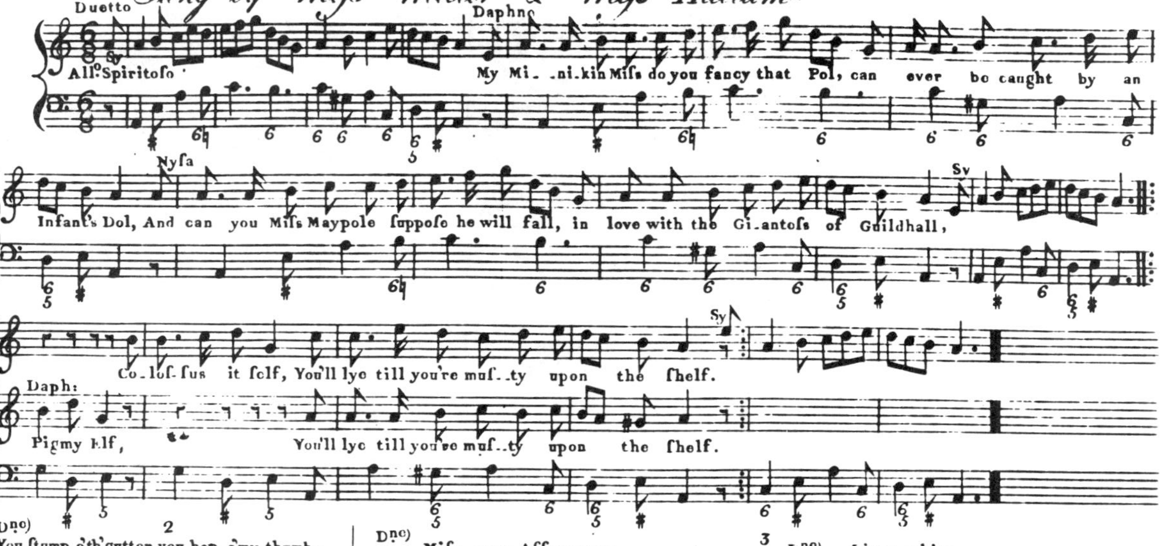
Duetto
Allº Spiritoso
Daphne
My Mi..ni.kin Miss do you fancy that Pol, can ever be caught by an
Nysa
Infant's Dol, And can you Miss Maypole suppose he will fall, in love with the Gi..antess of Guildhall,
Sy
Co..los..sus it self, You'll lye till you're mus..ty upon the shelf.
Daph:
Pigmy Elf, You'll lye till you're mus..ty upon the shelf.

2

Dne)
You stump o'th'gutter you hop o'my thumb,
A Husband for you must from Lilliput come,
Na) You stalking steeple you gawky stag,
Your Husband must come from Brobdignag.
Dne Sour Grapes,
Na Lead Apes,
Both) I'll humble your Vanity Mistress Trapes.

Dne) Miss your Assurance,
Na) And Miss your high Airs,
Dne) Is past all indurance,
Na) Are at their last Pray'rs.
Dne) No more of those freedoms Miss Nysa I beg,
Na) Miss Daphne's conceit must be lower'd a Peg,
Dne) Poor Spite.
Na) Pride hurt.

3

Dne) Liver white.
Na) Rare Sport.
Dne) Do shew your teeth spite fire do but you cant bite,
Na) This haughtiness soon will be laid in the Dirt,
Poor Spite. &c.
Pride hurt. &c.

Sung by Mr. Dunstall
Pan
Sy
A Pox of your pother about this or that, your shrieking or squeaking a
Sharp or a Flat, I'm Sharp by my bumpers, you're Flat Master Pol, so here goes a set to at Toll de roll loll de roll toll de roll de roll toll de roll
loll de roll toll de roll loll de roll toll de roll loll.
(2)
When Beauty her pack of poor Lovers would hamper,
And after Miss Will o'the Whisp the fools Scamper;
Ding dong, in Sing Song, they the Lady extol,
Pray what's all this fuss for but Toll de roll &c.
(3)
Mankind are a Medley _ a chance Medley race,
All start in full Cry to give dame Fortune Chace;
There's Catch as Catch can, hit or Miss luck is all,
And luck's the best Tune of Life's Toll loll de roll &c.
(4)
I've done please your Worship 'tis rather too long,
I only meant Life is but an Old Song;
The Worlds but a Tragedy Comedy, droll,
Where all Act the Scene of Toll loll de roll &c.
Sung by Mr. Mattocks
Pol
Pizzicato
Ah happy hours how fleeting how fleeting, ye

(2)
But from her Charms when sunder'd,
As MIDAS frowns presage,
Each hour will seem an hundred,
Each Day appear an Age.

Sung by Miss Hallam, Miss Miller, Miss Poitier, Mr. Beard, Mr. Mattocks, & Mr. Fawcett.

Pol

Dunce, I did but sham, for Apollo I am, God of Music & King of Parnas, thy scurvy decree for Pan against me, I reward with the Ears of an Ass, an Ass, I re-ward with the Ears of an Ass.

Chorus

Mysis Dam: Midas

Detected baulk'd & small, on our marrow bones we fall, be Merciful, be Pitiful, forgive us mighty Sol.

Adagio

Cho: Apollo

Alass, Alass, Thou a Billinsgate Queen, thou a Pander obscene, with strumpets & Baliffs shall class, Thou driven from Man, shalt wander with Pan, he a stinking old Goat, you an Ass, an Ass, he a stinking old Goat you an Ass.

Daph: Nysa Sil:

Now my Heart's cur'd of folly, be Jolly, the

Daph:
Nysa
Cho:
Oracles word for Millions shou'd pass, Mysis well parted, And the pimp Carted, Squire Midas converted into an Ass, O the dull Ass.
Apollo
Be thou Squire - his Estate, to you I translate, to you his strong Chests wicked Mass, Live happy while I, recall'd to the Sky, make all the Gods
laugh at Mida a a a as, make all the Gods laugh at Midas, laugh at Midas.
Cho:
To the
Nysa
bright God of Day, let us Sing, Dance, & Play, clap hands ev'ry Lad with his Lass. Now Criticks lie snug not a hiss groan or shrug remember the fate of Midas, Mi-
Cho:
das, remember the fate of Midas. Now Criticks lie snug, not a hiss groan or shrug, remember the fate of Midas, Midas, remember the fate of Midas.

THE AUGUSTAN REPRINT SOCIETY

William Andrews Clark Memorial Library
UNIVERSITY OF CALIFORNIA, LOS ANGELES

2520 Cimarron Street (at West Adams), Los Angeles, California 90018

Publications of the first fifteen years of the Society (numbers 1–90) are available in paperbound units of six issues at $16.00 per unit, from the Kraus Reprint Company, 16 East 46th Street, New York, N.Y. 10017.

Publications in print are available at the regular membership rate of $5.00 for individuals and $8.00 for institutions per year. Prices of single issues may be obtained upon request. Subsequent publications may be checked in the annual prospectus.

Make check or money order payable to

THE REGENTS OF THE UNIVERSITY OF CALIFORNIA

The Augustan Reprint Society

PUBLICATIONS IN PRINT

1948-1949

16. Henry Nevil Payne, *The Fatal Jealousie* (1673).
18. "Of Genius," in *The Occasional Paper*, Vol. III, No. 10 (1719), and Aaron Hill, Preface to *The Creation* (1720).

1949-1950

19. Susanna Centlivre, *The Busie Body* (1709).
20. Lewis Theobald, *Preface to the Works of Shakespeare* (1734).
22. Samuel Johnson, *The Vanity of Human Wishes* (1749), and two *Rambler* papers (1750).
23. John Dryden, *His Majesties Declaration Defended* (1681).

1951-1952

26. Charles Macklin, *The Man of the World* (1792).
31. Thomas Gray, *An Elegy Wrote in a Country Churchyard* (1751), and *The Eton College Manuscript.*

1952-1953

41. Bernard Mandeville, *A Letter to Dion* (1732).

1964-1965

109. Sir William Temple, *An Essay Upon the Original and Nature of Government* (1680).
110. John Tutchin, *Selected Poems* (1685-1700).
111. *Political Justice* (1736).
113. T. R., *An Essay Concerning Critical and Curious Learning* (1698).
114. Two Poems Against Pope: Leonard Welsted, *One Epistle to Mr. A. Pope* (1730); and *The Blatant Beast* (1742).

1965-1966

115. Daniel Defoe and others, *Accounts of the Apparition of Mrs. Veal.*
116. Charles Macklin, *The Convent Garden Theatre* (1752).
117. Sir Roger L'Estrange, *Citt and Bumpkin* (1680).
118. Henry More, *Enthusiasmus Triumphatus* (1662).
119. Thomas Traherne, *Meditations on the Six Days of the Creation* (1717).
120. Bernard Mandeville, *Aesop Dress'd or a Collection of Fables* (1740).

1966-1967

123. Edmond Malone, *Cursory Observations on the Poems Attributed to Mr. Thomas Rowley* (1782).
124. *The Female Wits* (1704).
125. *The Scribleriad* (1742). Lord Hervey, *The Difference Between Verbal and Practical Virtue* (1742).

1968-1969

133. John Courtenay, *A Poetical Review of the Literary and Moral Character of the Late Samuel Johnson* (1786).
134. John Downes, *Roscius Anglicanus* (1708).
135. Sir John Hill, *Hypochondriasis, a Practical Treatise* (1766).
136. Thomas Sheridan, *Discourse . . . Being Introductory to His Course of Lectures on Elocution and the English Language* (1759).
137. Arthur Murphy, *The Englishman From Paris* (1736).

1969-1970

138. [Catherine Trotter] *Olinda's Adventures* (1718).
139. John Ogilvie, *An Essay on the Lyric Poetry of the Ancients* (1762).
140. *A Learned Dissertation on Dumpling* (1726) and *Pudding Burnt to Pot or a Compleat Key to the Dissertation on Dumpling* (1727).
141. Selections from Sir Roger L'Estrange's *Observator* (1681-1687).
142. Anthony Collins, *A Discourse Concerning Ridicule and Irony in Writing* (1729).
143. *A Letter From A Clergyman to His Friend, With An Account of the Travels of Captain Lemuel Gulliver* (1726).
144. *The Art of Architecture, A Poem. In Imitation of Horace's Art of Poetry* (1742).

1970-1971

145-146. Thomas Shelton, *A Tutor to Tachygraphy, or Short-writing* (1642) and *Tachygraphy* (1647).

147-148. *Deformities of Dr. Samuel Johnson* (1782).

149. *Poeta de Tristibus: or the Poet's Complaint* (1682).
150. Gerard Langbaine, *Momus Triumphans: or the Plagiaries of the English Stage* (1687).

1971-1972

151-152. Evan Lloyd, *The Methodist. A Poem* (1766).

153. *Are these Things So?* (1740), and *The Great Man's Answer to Are these Things So?* (1740).

154. Arbuthnotiana: *The Story of the St. Alb-ns Ghost* (1712), and *A Catalogue of Dr. Arbuthnot's Library* (1779).

155-156. A Selection of Emblems from Herman Hugo's *Pia Desideria* (1624), with English Adaptations by Francis Quarles and Edmund Arwaker.

1972-1973

157. William Mountfort, *The Life and Death of Doctor Faustus* (1697).

158. Colley Cibber, *A Letter from Mr. Cibber, to Mr. Pope* (1742).

159. [Catherine Clive], *The Case of Mrs. Clive* (1744).

160. [Thomas Tryon], *A Discourse . . . of Phrensie, Madness or Distraction* from *A Treatise of Dreams and Visions* [1689].

161. Robert Blair, *The Grave. A Poem* (1743).

162. Bernard Mandeville, *A Modest Defence of Publick Stews* (1724).

Publications of the first fifteen years of the Society (numbers 1-90) are available in paperbound units of six issues at $16.00 per unit. from the Kraus Reprint Company, 16 East 46th Street, New York, N.Y. 10017.

Publications in print are available at the regular membership rate of $5.00 for individuals and $8.00 for institutions per year. Prices of single issues may be obtained upon request. Subsequent publications may be checked in the annual prospectus.

Make check or money order payable to

THE REGENTS OF THE UNIVERSITY OF CALIFORNIA

and send to

The William Andrews Clark Memorial Library
2520 Cimarron Street, Los Angeles, California 90018